CATERINA PIGORINI BERI

SACRED AND **PROFANE** TATTOOS OF THE HOLY HOUSE OF LORETO

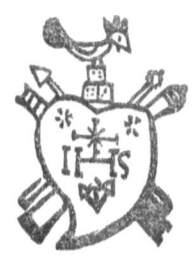

ALBERO NIRO EDITORE

Sacred and Profane Tattoos of the Holy House of Loreto
Translation: Alessandra Borroni
2018 © Alessandra Borroni
aleborroni@alice.it

Original edition:
Tatuaggi Sacri e Profani della Santa Casa di Loreto
by Caterina Pigorini-Beri
Original Edition:
Lapi editore -1889 - Città di Castello

Thanks for the help in translating
to Emanuela Curci and Adam Frieze

Total or partial reproduction of the text
is forbidden by any means without
prior consent in writing by the translator.

ISBN: 9781983097348
Indipendetly published

TABLE OF CONTENTS

Preface 7
Sacred and Profane Tattoos
of the Holy House of Loreto 11
Tattoos of the Francescanian order 33
Society of Jesus Tattoos 37
Tattoos of the two orders 45
Various religious tattoos 49
Loving Tattoos 55
Tattoos of young brides,
sailors and widows 57
Biography of the author 59

PREFACE
by Alessandra Borroni

I am particularly attached to the tradition of the sacred tattoos even though I have no sign engraved on my skin.

The sacred tattoo goes beyond any ritual of religious tradition, spontaneously arises from the people by telling a strong need for belonging and faith. Caterina Pigorini Beri at the end of 1800, living in the Marche region and being fascinated by its traditions, writes the book *Costumi e Superstizioni dell'Appennino Marchigiano* (1889). She dedicates part of this book to the tradition that developed in the 15th century around the Holy House of Loreto.

The Holy House arrived on the Marche coast in 1294, in the following centuries its great fame and veneration was so popular that it led pilgrims and devotees from all over Europe. These pilgrims set off on long and treacherous paths to reach it.

Right here, after the journey of faith, the wayfarers made a mark engraved on the skin. Often the design represented an image linked to devotion but over time also spread. These significant symbols were anchors, hearts, skulls, etc.

Few were the families of "markers" who were around the Holy House to tattoo the pilgrims, they had a small "catalogue" of available designs that could be engraved on the skin through steel "pens" and indigo blue pigment. The boxwood tablets with which the design was sketched are still preserved in the Museo Antico Tesoro of the Holy House of Loreto.

Perhaps the practice came in this territory from the tradition of the tattoos that had developed among the Crusaders. It was mark of recognition of Christianity for the soldiers. This assured them a ecclesistic burial; or the tradition could be traced back to the imitation of the stigmata received by Saint Francis a few centuries earlier in La Verna.

After centuries of practice the tradition of tattooing was forbidden. Although in part it continued underground, so much so that until a few decades ago it was still possible to meet in the countryside of the Marche some peasants with an indigo symbol engraved on their wrist or forearm. One of these peasants was my great-grandmother.

SACRED AND PROFANE TATTOOS OF THE HOLY HOUSE OF LORETO
by Caterina Pigorini Beri

In going collecting the superstitions, fairy tales, legends and beliefs of the Marche Apennines, I was impressed by a unique costumance that is found in almost all the populations of the ancient Piceno, enclosed between the Adriatic sea and the river Tronto, the Umbria and the Abruzzi.

This population is so simple, kind and intelligent in which it seems that the Umbrian and Etruscan civilizations have been confused and almost rested. The inhabitants had the use of tattooing; men individually: and it is easy to discover it, because in general they tattooed their arms towards your wrist.

The observer is surprised to see the peasants with the sleeves rolled up, these symbolic signs of turquoise colour: a figure, a motto, a cross and the symbols of the Passion, with the sun and the moon, or that of the Holy Spirit, and one or two hearts above a globe, also sometimes a star; then a thousandth, eternal, unerasable *forget-me-not,* as the song says.

This is so natural and it is so common that it is not even mentioned. In fact nobody, that I know, in the country has ever mentioned this strange custom, particular to a region, which must necessarily have an ethnographic and historical importance of the first order.

Following the scientific investigation and looking for the reason of such a peculiar custom, which has become so common that it does not even attract the attention of those who are subject to study tattoos of the barbaric and primitive populations and those of the jails and other mysteries and very unhappy places, I managed not only to know where and from whom these tattoos are practiced, but I also came into possession of almost a hundreds of ancient clichés in fruit wood, perhaps engraved with a nail, and two awl or pens, with which the colour of the strange hieroglyphs is injected into the living flesh.

The bizarre and unexpectedly collection found - and of which I am pleased to be able to present the authentic engravings - is the result of a seizure that occurred until the beginning of our Risorgimento[1]. In that period the civil wisdom of the rulers investigated and sought with love and faith the attitudes, customs, hatred and love of the redeemed peoples, to oppose every evil remedy, to every guilt a punishment, to every misfortune a relief. This kidnapping was made to a gravedigger; social class which, despite the work of mercy entrusted to it, is kept in great dismay by the Piceno population, and which is very likely to continue to exercise this illegal activity, because the pilgrims of the Marche still continue to have tattoos.

Everyone knows the legend of the pious House of

---

1 Period leading to unification of Italy, around 1815 – 1871

Nazareth, who fleeing the persecution of the Turks. It left between Istria and Dalmatia to the city of Fiume[2]: and then, reigning His Holiness Pope Boniface VIII, and precisely on the night of December 10th 1294, the Holy House crossed the Adriatic sea, and settled on a hill owned by two Antici brothers, who, having seen the great quantity of the offerings of the faithful, were tempted and seemed to be they also asked themselves: *In templo quid fecit aurum?* (trans. What's gold doing in a church?). They sought the solution in the manner of Cain and Abel, *brothers knives*, as the proverb of the Marche says.

It was a bad scandal; so that before the pope defined the dispute and that it stood above the majestic temple, which makes it one of the most beautiful monuments of Christianity, the House cut off the

---

2   See in this regard the unique book of Montaigne - *Journal du voyage en Italie* - published by Alessandro D'Ancona, with illustrative notes that are for themselves a book (Lapi, Città di Castello, 1889). The Montaigne mentions this pilgrimage species of the Schiavoni. Himself then, despite steps for the initiator of the new philosophy, did not disdain to take part in it. - Beyond that he says: "*"J'y peus trouver a toute peine place, et avec beaucoup de faveur, pour y loger un tableau dans lequel il y a quatre figures d'arjant attachées: cele de notre Dame, la miene, cele de ma feme, cele de ma fille. Au pied de la miene, il y a insculpé sur l'arjant: Michael Montanus, Gallus Vasco, Eques Regij Ordinis,1581: a cele de ma fame: Francisca Cassaniana uxor : a cele de ma fille: Leonora Montana filia unica: et sont tontes de ranc a genous dans ce tableau, et la Notre Dame en haut au devant.*"

It's useless to seek today the vow offered by the author of the Essais at the Lauretano Sanctuary, which being silver will have been melted together with others and perhaps minted, since it is not, as D'Ancona, that existed more in 1792, before the French confiscation and depredation.

Moreover, it would have been a very unusual human document to offer this to the Shirne of the capricious moralist, who preceded the Cartesian philosophy, and thus opened the way to modern thought for the first in France.

question, and settled in a forest of Madonna Lauretta, or rather, as you wish, in a forest of laurels, who bowed to the ground around it, from which the name Loreto would be derived - if we did not want to follow the etymology of Vittoria Colonna who in her letter in favor of the Capuchins, to whom the temple is confided, calls it *Madonna dell'Oreto* (trans. Our Lady of the golden place).

The struggle of the two Antici brothers, that fight for the gold of the temple, is depicted in the shell of the Holy House carved in Carrara marble by Sansovino, Sangallo, Bandinelli, Raffallo da Montelupo, together with the history of the Virgin, the Passion, the translation, the prophets and the sibyls. All of which made go into raptures Canova[3], he advised his students to go in the times of vacation to inspire them on those walls.

We can see that the *Sacra auri fames*[4] was an habit of the Antici family, because by atavism it descended also into the mother of that Giacomo Leopardi[5]. Poet to whom the blue mountains, not

---

[3] Antonio Canova (1757 – 1822) was an Italian Neoclassical sculptor, famous for his marble sculptures. Often regarded as the greatest of the Neoclassical artists, his artwork was inspired by the Baroque and the classical revival, but avoided the melodramatics of the former, and the cold artificiality of the latter. (from *Wikipedia*)

[4] The accursed greed for gold. An expression that voices St. Paul's dictum that the desire of money is the root of all evil. (from www.catholicculture.org)

[5] Giacomo Leopardi (1798 – 1837) was an Italian philosopher, poet, essayist, and philologist. He is widely seen as one of the most radical and challenging thinkers of the 19th century. Although he lived in a secluded town in the conservative Papal States, he came in touch with the main ideas of the Enlightenment, and through his own literary evolution, created a remarkable and renowned poetic work, related to the Romantic era. The strongly lyrical quality of his poetry

far from which rested the Holy House, they took away the sight of beautiful things, when arcane worlds, arcane happily to his life and that he had to feel as marveling the story of that translation, narrated by his father in such a way that the Church itself had to reject her.

Still now in the night from December 10th into the morning of the 11th, all the campaigns of Piceno around midnight, time of translation, ring bells continuously. There is a burst of mortars and gunshots that arouse the mountain and rejoice it; and from the Sibyl mountain to the port of San Benedetto del Tronto, from Chienti to the Esino, the whole Marche is on fire. No house is at the dark, as if you wanted to illuminate the way to the desired and wonderful House: the ancient bonfires light up, the fires of religious joy, and the praises of Mary are sung, which sometimes are alternated with loving songs.

Maria piccina
La dico ogni mattina
Ogni mattina la dirò
In paradiso ci anderò...

(Little Mary
I say it every morning
Every morning I'll say it
In heaven I will go...)

and so on; following by extraordinary things like this that has nothing to do with the Holy House:

made him a central figure on the European and international literary and cultural landscape. (from *Wikipedia*)

Quanto mi piace vestir turchino
Perché ci si veste l'onde dello mare.
E ci si veste pure la mentuccia
Verde la rama e turchinella tutta:
E ci si veste pure lo mentone
Verde la rama e truchino lo fiore!

Ho fatto un pianto accosto alla marina
Pure li pesci ho fatti lagrimare:
Me l'hanno detto, povera meschina
sta penitenza chi te la fa fare:
Me la fa fare un giovane crudele
Che m'ha lasciata e non mi vuol più bene;
Me la fa fare un giovane vivace
Che m'ha lasciata e non vuol far la pace.

(How much I like to dress turquoise
Because so dress the waves of the sea.
And so dress the pennyroyal too
Green the branch and turquoise whole:
And so dress the wild mint too
Green the branch and turquoise the flower!

I cried near the sea,
I made cry even the fishes:
They told me, poor unhappy
who makes you do this penance?
A cruel young man makes me do it
who left me and doesn't love me anymore
a lively young man makes me do it
who has left me and does not want to make peace with me.)

In this alternative of love and pain, of worship and passion, we also include the loving tattoos mixed in the long crown of tablets engraved with images of God and the Virgin.

The pilgrimage to Loreto for the feast of the Nativity of the Virgin in September, is a mixture of young people. Girls are dressed in gala, with traditional corals, the wide hoop earrings with stars jingle at the ears, and the red handkerchief tied like a turban. Those wagons with many seats called *cacciatore* are pulled by the patient donkeys and adorned of red bows against envy (*the evil eye*) or on the *birocci*[6], to which the oxen are moored with the bright decoration. These oxen are held in the grip and led to reins by the herdsman, who will adorn his hat with a beautiful palm[7] bought and blessed in the Holy House. This various, mixed pilgrimage, that stops at night, to camp outside, ahead of the temple, as in the Mecca, is almost all a loving pilgrimage: a raw poetry, primitive, full of charms and splendors, which deserves the brush of Michetti and the pen of De Amici.

The *ciociari*[8] are mixed with the people from Abruzzo, Umbria and Marche. In a long periods of time Istrian and Dalmatians[9] descend with their lament, because the Holy House left from there, and

---

6   Two or four-wheeled cart pulled by animals for transporting things.
7   Little olive branch, traditionally regarded as a symbol of peace (in allusion to the story of Noah in Gen. 8:1, in which a dove returns with an olive branch after the Flood).
8   People from Ciociaria, region of Central Italy roughly corresponding to the province of Frosinone.
9   People from Istria and Dalmazia, regions located in Croazia at the east shores of the Adriatic sea.

like the Albanians of the south of Italy facing East sing: *O bella Morea, dacchè ti ho lasciata più non ti vidi* (Tras. O beautiful Morea, since I left you no longer I saw you), they sing piously:

Ritorna a noi, bella Signora,
Ritoma a noi, Maria.
Colla tua casa!

(Come back to us, beautiful Lady,
Come back to us, Mary,
with your house!)

Then the pilgrimage breaks: part goes to Assisi, part to Sirolo, or rather to Umana[10], where there is the Crucifix of Sirolo, as says in the popular adage:

Chi va a Loreto e non va a Sirolo
Vede la Madre e non il Figliolo

(Who goes to Loreto and doesn't go to Sirolo
he sees the Mother and not the Son)

This *Crucifix of Sirolo*, highly reproduced on the flesh of the devoted pilgrims, singular because it is dressed like the one mentioned by St. Gregory of Tours and like the other of St. Cosma and Damiano in Rome, in the that manifests its Greek origin: the incessant reproduction of the Passion and its emblems, but, more than anything, St. Francis

---

10   *Umana* is the ancient name of the village, today the name has changed to *Numana*, near Ancona.

with the stigmata, as it can be seen in the gross engraving, it has led me to a result that I believe conforms to the truth.

Scientific research has this attraction, which gives all things their reason to be, does not leave anyone concerned with it quiet, if only one link is missing in the chain of human harmonies.

No other sanctuary has so many tattoos (even if there are other shrines that have such a strange custom) as that of Loreto. A worthy fact of the highest attention is this that, the sacred tattoo of Loreto, without speaking for the moment about the *loving tattoos*, which are a direct consequence, have a singular variety of types and symbolic figures, which have nothing to do with the happy event of translation, which also rejoices so much the simple inhabitants of the Piceno.

We understand very well the engraving of the Virgin in all the symbols and in all the figures and as it may have relevance with it but even many more designs come out of the topic of the Holy House. We can find among the drawings: Saint Francis - who lived almost a century before the translation (*Tab. II, 11*); the emblems of the passion (*Tab. IX*); the Crucifix of Sirolo (*Tab. VIII, 10bis, 11,12bis*). This crucifix has an even more miraculous history, if it is possible, of the Holy House. The tradition assigns to it a century and a half of precedence over the convent of Sirolo, founded by St. Francis. This crucifix of which Nicodemus is the author, carried by Charlemagne, buried three centuries in the earth, whose miraculous ampoules of blood and water even took care of the Council of Nicaea. Two years after the translation, it was brought by the sea waves floating to Umana.

Going back to tattoo designs there are: St. Clare (*Tab. II, 12,13*), contemporary and fellow citizen of St. Francis, with the palm of virginity and the pyx in her hand - as she knew, being a woman, she could not touch the pyx - placed in the act of averting the imminent danger of the Saracen assault on her convent of the Poor Clares and exclaim the not won words: *Domine, ne tradis bestiis animas confitentes tibi* (Trans. Lord, doesn't give the lives of your faithful in the hands of these wild beasts). All these deigns are off from the topic of the Holy House.

Investigating in the traditions and legends of these peoples who possess true treasures of language, poetry and art, we can almost with certainly indicate how, why and when this sacred tattoos originated. It doesn't need to go far from the place where Fra' Jacopone and Saint Francis gave Italy the first maternal accent; from the known ascending to the unknown, and rummaging to torture poetry, legend and history.

The Friars Minor, in their oral legends, attribute to Saint Francis a prophecy in the form of an acrostic of the word *Picenum*. He would announced almost it a century before the translation of the Holy House. This prophecy, which I give as it was given to me, would have been made when the Saint left the beautiful valley that tore off gentle words from him: *Nil jucundius vidi valle mea Spoletana* (trans. I have not seen anything more joyful than my Spoleto valley), before retiring on the Alverno[11], where he received the stigmata. He went on the Conero (or Mount of Ancona), to find the convent of Sirolo, from which the crucifix of Umana takes its name, and looking towards the forest that was later of Madonna Lauretta, he uttered the word Picenum, illustrating it as follows:

P ortatur (it is brought)
J uxta (at)
C onerum (Conero)
E dicula (the little house)
N azarene (of the Nazareth)
V irginis (Virgin)
M arie (Mary)

So, it seems to me, that the sacred tattoos of Loreto owes its origin to the Stigmata of St. Francis in order to reproduce its symbol and the figure. It would be confirmed by the custom they have of tattooing in the forearm near the hand and also in the hand itself, in places where you can let out so much blood that is enough to inject the indigo ink into it.

Loreto's tattoo has an exclusively mystical origin; it can not be confused with the tattoos that come to us from primitive civilizations: it is what could be called an institution. And also the loving tat-

---

11   The actual name is La Verna. It is a mount located in the Tuscan Apennines. It is one of most famous and notorious Franciscan place. This is because at La Verna st.Francis, after a long time of praying and penitence, the September 17th 1224 received the Stigmas. After this miraculous event, even many years later, La Verna became a focal point of increasing pilgrimage, that brought the place to become the big religious destination.

too, which appears at first sight in the numerous engravings that arise, has the special character of an oath to God that could be summed up in the verses of Fra' Jacopone:

Quanto è al mondo m'invita ad amare
Bestie ed uccelli e pesci dentro il mare;
Ciò che è sotto all'abisso e sopra all'are.

(How much is in the world invites to love
Beasts and birds and fishes within the sea;
What is unde the abyss and above the air.)

And if truly the cause of this strange religious ceremony were to be attributed to the Saint's stigmata, one could almost certainly establish the time in which it began to practice it. It would have been under the pontificate of Sixtus V[12] of Marche origins, of the Order of St. Francis, son of Marianna da Camerino, where the first Capuchins convent was established by Caterina Cybo (1501-1557), they have for the highest honour to sweep the floor of the Loreto temple. He enlarged and magnified the Porziuncola church in Assisi. He enclosed the city of Loreto with walls and it is better to say that he renewed the Cavalieri Lauretani[13] (Lauretan Knights). He enlarged the Illyrian College, and es-

---

12   Pope Sixtus V or Xystus V (1521 – 1590), born Felice Peretti di Montalto, was Pope of the Catholic Church from 24 April 1585 to his death in 1590. As a youth, he joined the Franciscan order.
13   The Lauretan Knights were an Equestrian Order established in 1545 by Pope Paul III. The aim was to create a defense to the Holy House of Loreto to preserve it from attacks from land and sea, especially from pirate ships that raged in the Adriatic Sea.

tablished numerous privileges, which now does not matter to mention, to defend the Sanctuary from the invasions of the Turks, always threatening on the Adriatic area; which would also explain why the fishermen and sailors of the coast are preferably tattooed even today.

Comparisons patiently established in studying the rough engravings in relation to history, seem to affirm this timid opinion.

Pope Sixtus V, in establishing all the privileges for the city of Loreto, with the obligation to fight against the Turks, had established that the coat of arms of the city of Loreto was the Virgin sitting above the Holy House laid on three mountains between two branches of pear tree with the motto Felix Lauretana Civitas, thus symbolizing part of his coat of arms and his original name: Felice Peretti cardinal of Montalto. In the engravings we see the Virgin crowned by angels and supported by an entire plant of pesr with two big fruits on the top (*Tab. II, 14*)

The three distinct characters of this tattoo are remarkable. Other designs have been added over the years, how could prove the figure of Saint Filomena martyr (*Tab. X, 12*), discovered in this century in the catacombs of Rome, and the figure of the Immaculate Conception (*Tab. II, 16*), the eternal dream of the Franciscans, for which dogma was pronounced recently. The one that is primitive, original, in honor and similarity of the Stigmata of St. Francis (*Tab. I, 6*); from the Virgin of Loreto to the Crucifix of Sirolo; from the figure of the Cross to the signs of the Passion and to the Stigmata of the Saint; that of the Jesuits with the name of Mary, of Jesus, with the Sacred Heart, with the cross of the stripped Christ, and with the rays and halves of the Eye of God (Tab. V, 21), having shared with the Franciscan the main symbol of Loreto, the loving tattoos that has the hearts tied in chain or pierced, and the dove with the olive branch of peace, like Erminia that:

Sovente allor che sugli estivi ardori
Giacean le pecorelle all'ombra assise,
Sulle scorze dei faggi e degli allori
Segnò l'amato nome in mille guise.

Often then on the summer ardours
the little sheep lied in the shade relaxed,
On the peels of the beeches and laurels
He marked her lover in a thousand guises.

To the loving tattoos (*Tab. XI*) properly said, it keeps behind, beyond the seafaring (*Tab. XII*) that is immediately understood, that of the brides, with the figure of the Spirit, as a wish and a promise - And the Word became flesh, and dwelt among us - and the widow with the skull and the shin-bones on the cross, and the *Memento Mei* or *Memento Mori* engraved below (*Tab. XII*): this evidently more modern than that also for the form of letters, and for the concept of an almost romantic mysticism, like the one that inspired Saint Jeanne-Françoise Frémyotde Chantal, who after the death of her husband incised the name of Jesus (*IHS*) in her chest with a hot iron.

If you didn't want to give to the Lauretan tattoo, so particular and so unformed by all the tattoos, this reason of the stigmata to which we can logically attribute, we could not go beyond the last crusade and precisely after 1291, period in which the legend affirms the translation of Holy House from Dalmazia into the Piceno area: since in the time of the V and VI crusades, that is the same time of Saint Francis and Luis IX called the Saint, the House of Nazareth, according to tradition, had not yet crossed the sea, and as Loreto did not exist there could not be the Lauretan tattoos. And in this case it could be explained that the discipline of the Church, once rigorous in terms of burial, had among the great pains that affected heretics established the deprivation of the burial ecclesiastical, to those affected by injury or violent or sudden death did not wear any sign of religion.

Now the Lauretans in the possession of the House of Nazareth more than the others had to go to the East. It would have been natural to have this indelible mark imprinted, being exposed to the pitfalls of the Turks, not so much for the burial, but for the Turkish or hell not to prevail.

It would have been almost like Tau on the foreheads of the men that Ezekiel speaks of in his prophecies, when the six men came into the street, and each of them had an instrument of death, and there was also a man among them deressed in linen and hung on his hips an inkwell to write, to mark a Tau on the forehead of men who mourn and grieve for all the abominations. We know that only they were saved from the terrible command of the avenger God. "Slay utterly old and young, both maids and little children and women; but come not near any man upon whom is the mark; and begin at my sanctuary".

In any case, whatever the era to which it is to be attributed, these inductions are only the first historical investigation explaining the origin of the continuity of the Lauretan tattoo. For if it were judged at the outside its historical environment could give rise to singular errors and mislead the reserchers of anthropology, who applying the principles of positive science would move away from the truth.

It is essential that the absolute independence that is necessary for the pursuit of truth, and to heal us from the prejudice of infallibility and priorism is carried in the examination of moral.

Following this system scrupulously and with that perseverance of inquiry that can lead to the solution of this and other serious scientific and psychological problems, it was made a new and singular discovery that I dearly abandon to the researchers. One day the famous Franciscan, Father Augustine of Montefeltro, who filled the world with the fame of his eloquence, preached in Rome in the church of San Carlo al Corso. In that church there was an immense crowd of people of all conditions and ages, but singularly the guilds of the regular and secular clergy to listen his words. In that crowd I observed a college of missionary priests with characteristic oriental figures, and several of them had tattooed hands. The instinct of the investigation dragged me close to them and led me to make a speech, that the zeal of a bigot, more papal by the Pope, cut me off in the middle, inspiring those modest heroes of a sublime idea and admirable, the scrupulous indiscretion on my part.

But the dialogue was not brutally cut off. I had not known before from one of them that he was a native of Beyrut, the village of the Crucifix of Sirolo, and his companion who stood beside Damascus, who came to Rome perhaps with the Irish missionaries, and indeed they spoke English, to learn and profess the Catholic apostolate there and then preach it in the language of the country to the infidels.

Now, the figures that those missionaries had in their hands were two. One could not decipher because of the scrupulous interruptions of the zealous Catholic, who did not allow those good ecclesiastics to abandon me their innocent hand, but the other was a Turkish scimitar which stood out of turquoise color on the bronze skin. The pious told me fleetingly that these drawings were the games that the Italians were doing when they went to holy places.

Evidently he and his tattooed companions were born Maometthians and those figures represented the stigma of their religion, before baptism erased with sin the original worship. That "game" of the Italians was like the stamp, the label of the race, which most likely imposes itself on them to distinguish those who were born Christians from those who are redeemed.

But this then proves something more: that the

tattoo practiced on the hands by Beyrut in Damascus and finally in the holy places is not indigenous, but imported; it is imported by Italians, who go there as pilgrimage as missionaries. Also benefiting my modest hypothesis on the Stigmata of St. Francis to note that the Holy Sepulcher and all the places consecrated by the Christian religion are kept and officiated by the Franciscans.

The tattoo of Loreto is practiced with a simple process that matters, however, to describe. Tinted somewhat and applied the rough engraving on the meat and narrow and tightened so that the imprint remains, with incredible speed the operator using a pen formed by three sharp steel attached to a handle with a big thread legation, he marks the contours with thick dots. Just finished, he stretches the skin of the patient on each side until the blood comes out of it. Then he smears a indigo ink on it that penetrates and settles forever, leaving exactly the drawing.

The operation is painful, but after twenty-four hours the pain is no longer felt.

The least tattooed I believe are inhabitants of the village of Loreto, as happens everywhere and in all things, which, in the likeness of the voice that needs the echo to grow, gain faith and intensity from the distance.

The large possessions of the Holy House have a real population of farmers who are certainly among the most beautiful of the Marche: especially women with bright black hair and black eyes . The peasant of the Holy House retain a special costume: dressed in black twill, often with the waistcoat that carry on the guazzarone15[14] which you can see the sleeves and lower flaps, breeches buttoned up to the ankle, held tight instead of the buckle and the strap, by a red ribbon on the kidneys and the cone-shaped hat, remind the Calabrian populations. So are the women, dressed in vivid colours, often without the corset with the engraved copper decoration, the wide swollen sleeves and the dress with thick pleated, like the Albanians.

They bring the large foodstuffs to their new landowners, remembrance of their ancestors, when in the wine cellars of the Holy House they brought the must for the historic and colossal barrels, and the wheat in the palace of Bramante, for the charity to the poors. They had free medicines from the pharmacy, where the vases were painted by Raffaello da Monte Lupo and they listen to the pacts and orders of His Holiness, dictated by their fellow citizen Traiano Boccalini, who was the skeptical and wise interpreter in the rooms covered with paintings by Guercino and Guido Reni, with curtains that were tapestries designed by Raffaello and Giulio Romano.

This legend, this story, this mystical and enchanting ceremony, which has inherited with the soil, which has been breathed in the aura of those delightful hills, has always been great importance for the legislator and the philosopher.

Today it acquired a much greater one, because it was able to give documents to experimental science.

Which, in the search for the reasons for human

---

[14] A garment of cloth, similar to a tunic, which men wore during labor in the fields, as a fatigue suit.

things, can not conceal itself, the eternal, the constant, the insatiable thirst that man has of the ideal.

Whether he climbs flying the clear heights of science, whether it bathes its blood the inhosts and savages that represent the new promised land of civilization: whether it descend under the earth to seek the secret of his birth faith, or ask the invisible world that of the vengeance of the immensely small against the immensely great; whether he seeks in his heart the reasons for his inquietude with implacable curiosity, or is imprinted in the flesh the sign of redeemed humanity or of the love that was the cause, origin and fulfillment; man always the same under the sun, tears in the sky the spark from heaven as Prometheus or the lightning like Franklin, can't help but look up and seek faith and hope in it, to idealize his destinies, and to lift his spirit above prose and vulgarity of life.

DRAWINGS
OF THE ORIGINAL
TATTOOS

TATTOOS OF
THE FRANCISCAN ORDER

Figures I

Symbols of Eucharistic sacrament

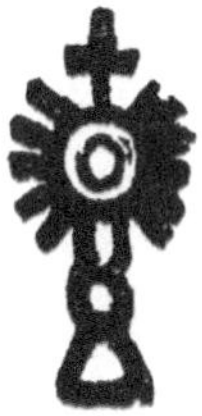

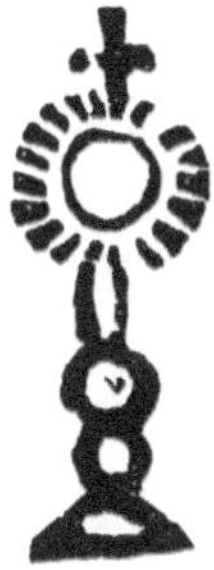

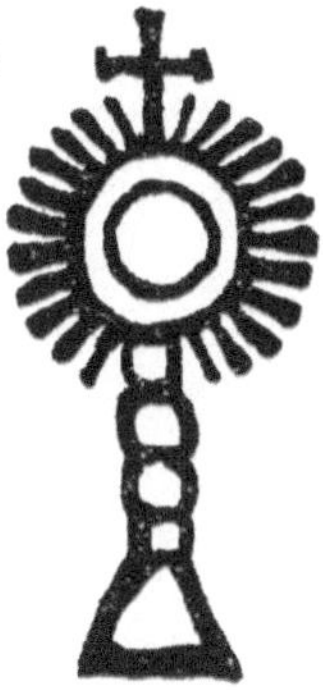

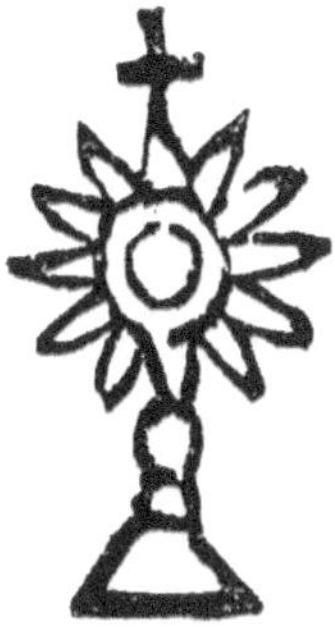

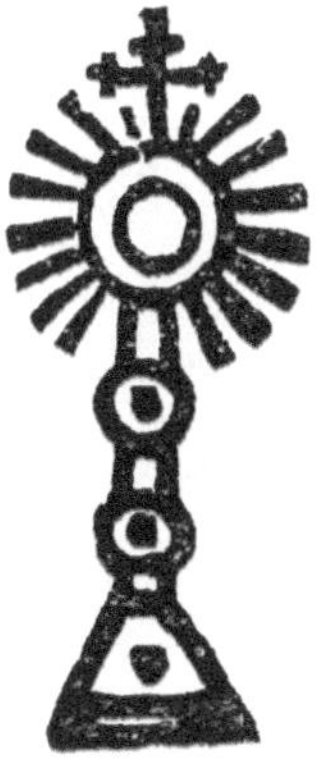

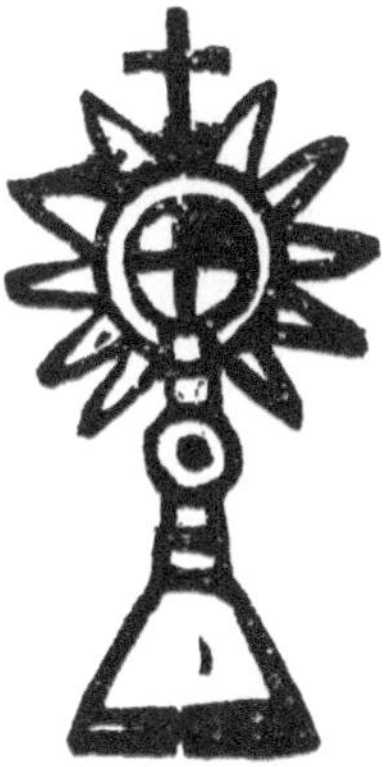

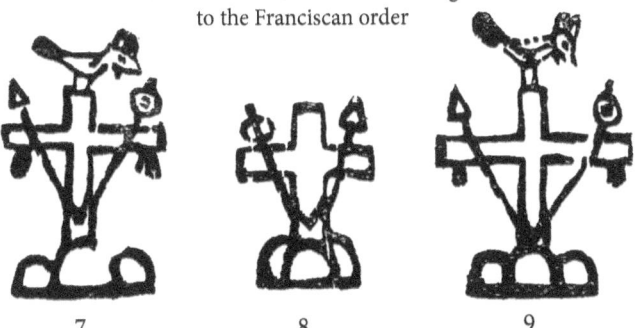

Emblems of the Passion according to the Franciscan order

TATTOOS ATTRIBUTED TO
THE FRANCISCAN ORDER

Figures II

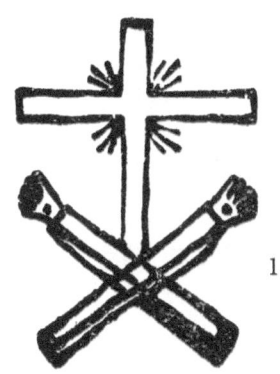

Symbol of the Franciscan order

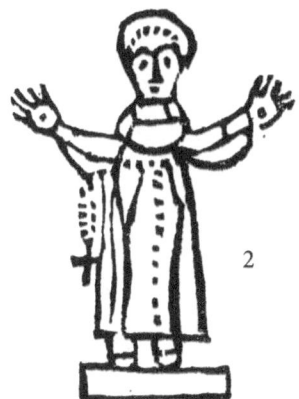

Saint Francis with the stigmata and the rosary

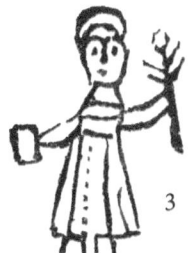

St. Clare with the palm and the pyx

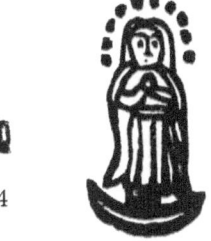

Immaculate Conception

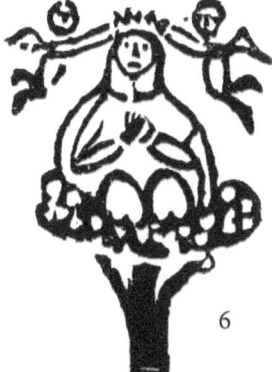

Madonna of the angels with part of the coat of arms of Sixtus V

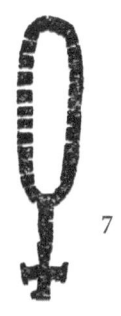

Rosary of Saint Francis

TATTOOS ATTRIBUTED TO
THE SOCIETY OF JESUS

Figures III

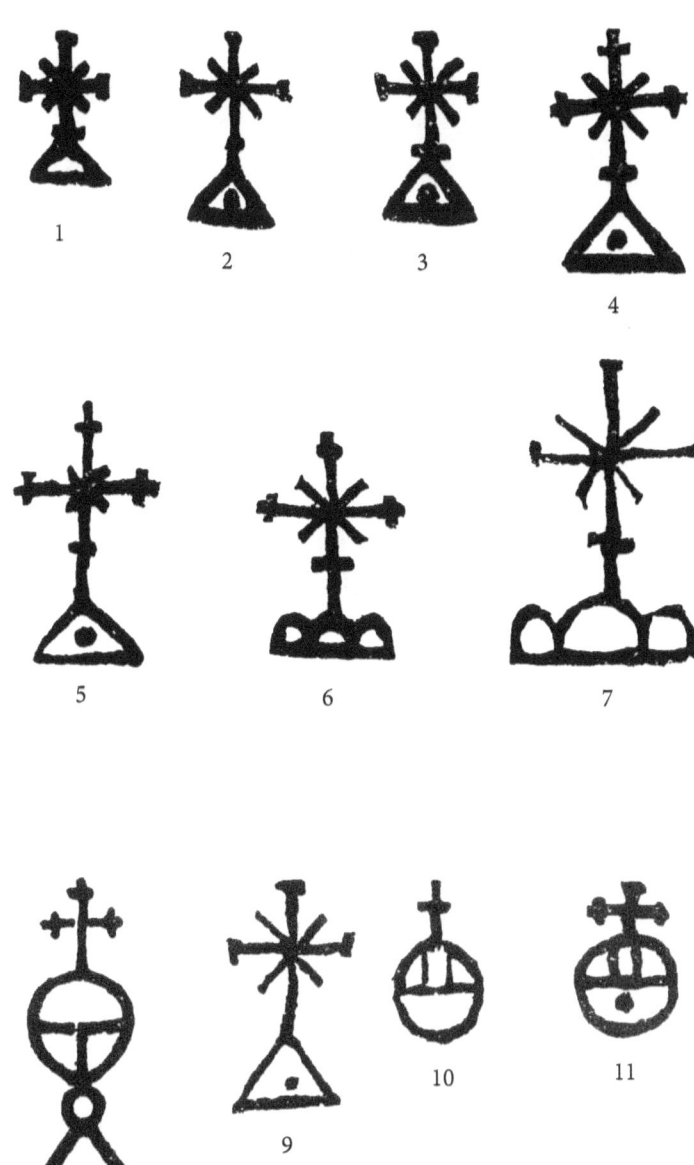

TATTOOS ATTRIBUTED TO
THE SOCIETY OF JESUS

Figures IV

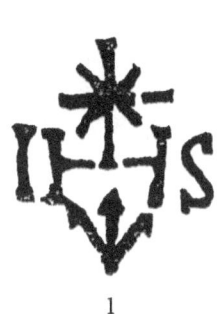

1

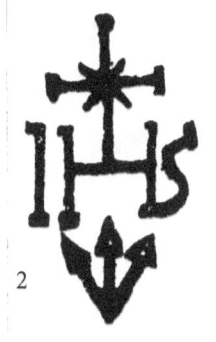

2

Cristogramma symbol
of the Company of Jesus

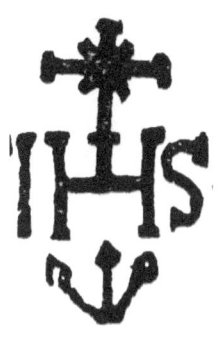

3

4

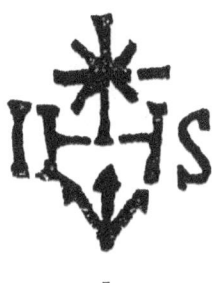

5

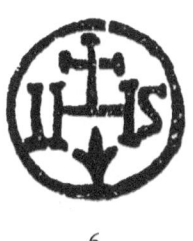

6

All-seeing eye
of God

7

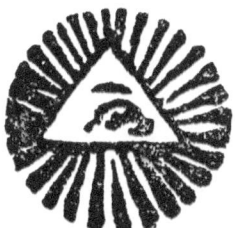

8

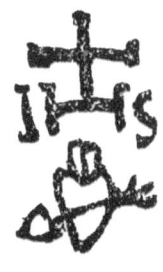

9

TATTOOS ATTRIBUTED TO THE SOCIETY OF JESUS

Figures V

Symbol of the Eucharistic sacrament

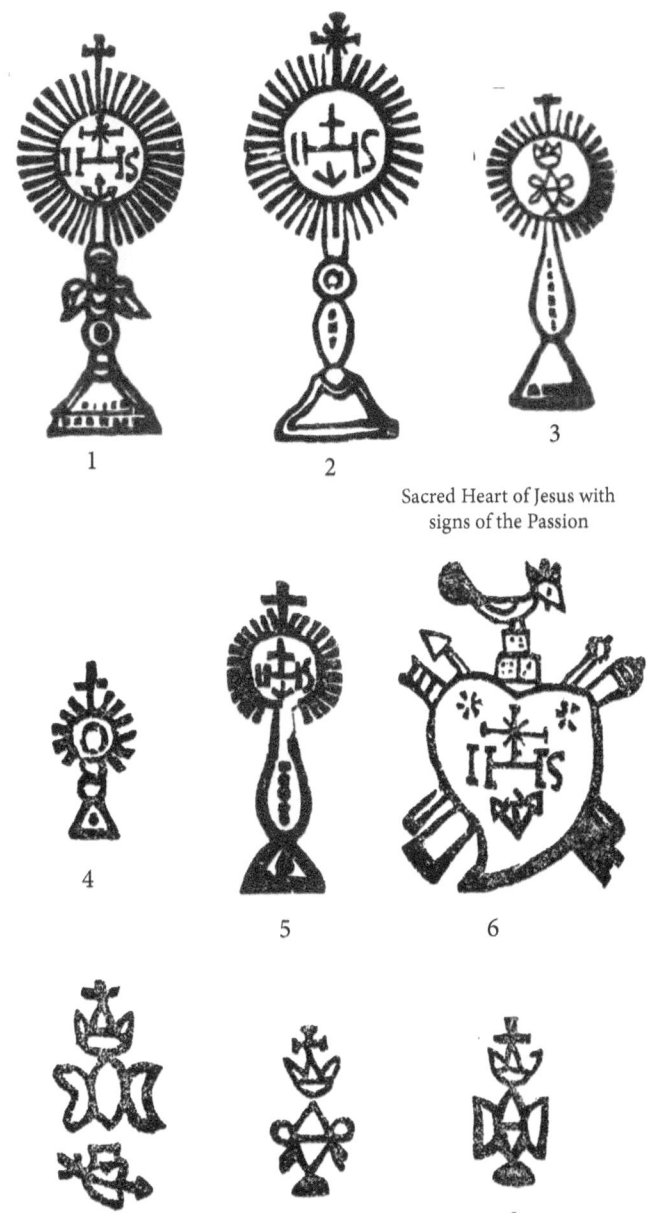

Sacred Heart of Jesus with signs of the Passion

41

TATTOOS ATTRIBUTED TO
THE SOCIETY OF JESUS

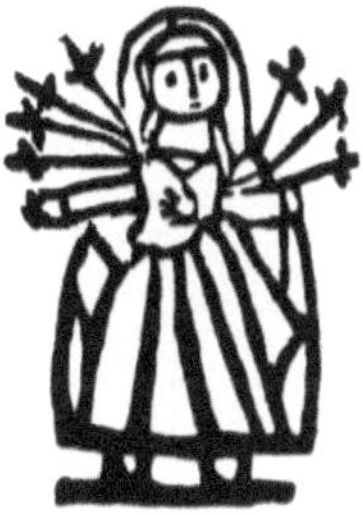

Figures VI

1

2

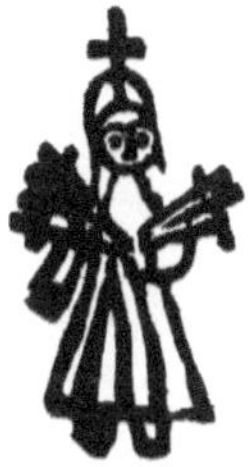

Virgin Mary of Seven Sorrows

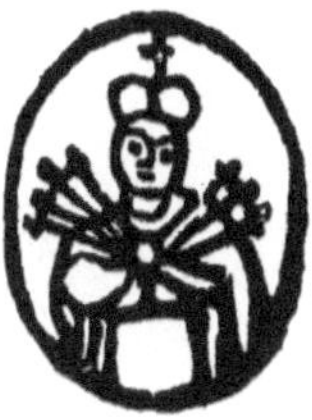

3

Our Lady of Sorrows

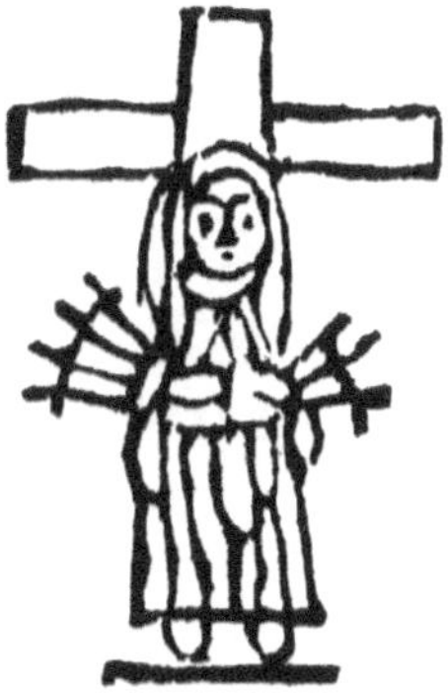

4

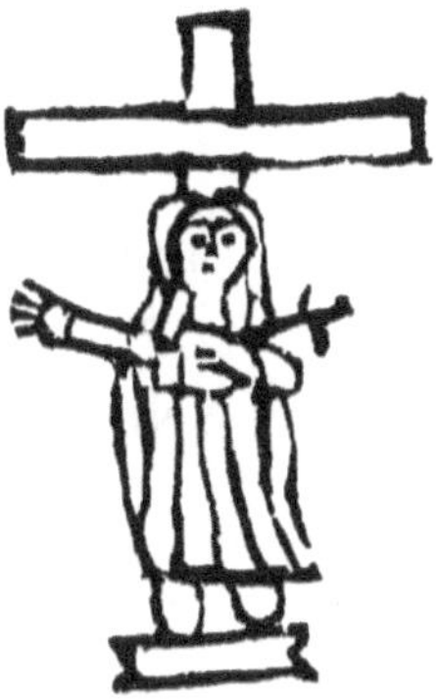

5

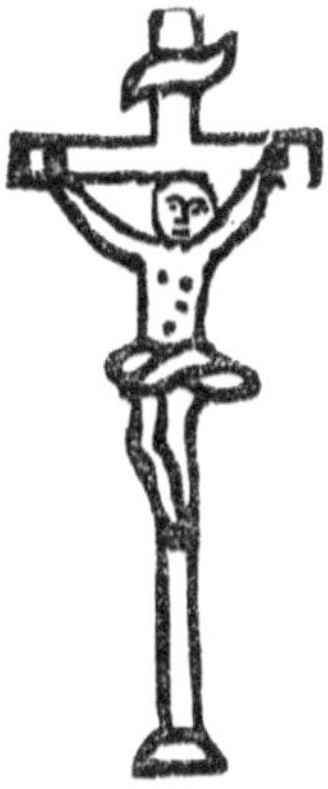

Our Lady of Sorrows

6

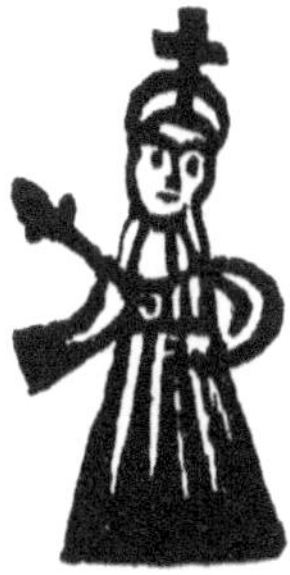

7

Sacred heart of Mary

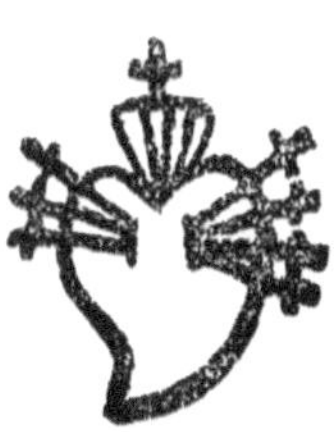

8

TATTOOS ATTRIBUTED TO
THE FRANCISCAN ORDER
AND THE SOCIETY OF JESUS

Figures VII

Our Lady of Loreto with Child

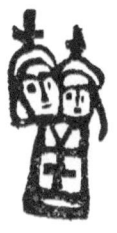
1

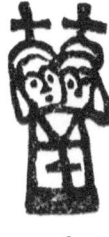
2

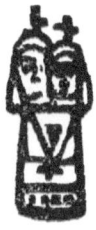
3

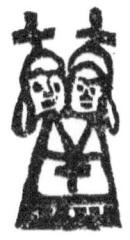
4

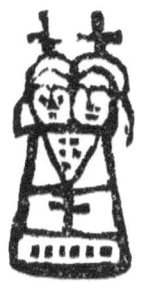
5

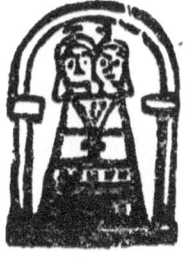
6

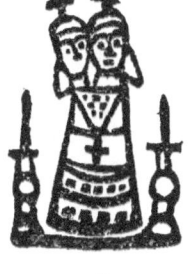
7

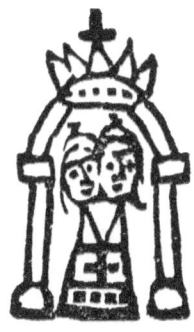
8

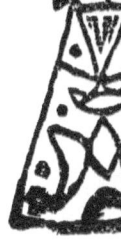
9

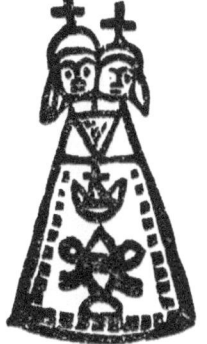
10

TATTOOS ATTRIBUTED TO
THE FRANCISCAN ORDER
AND THE SOCIETY OF JESUS

Figures VIII

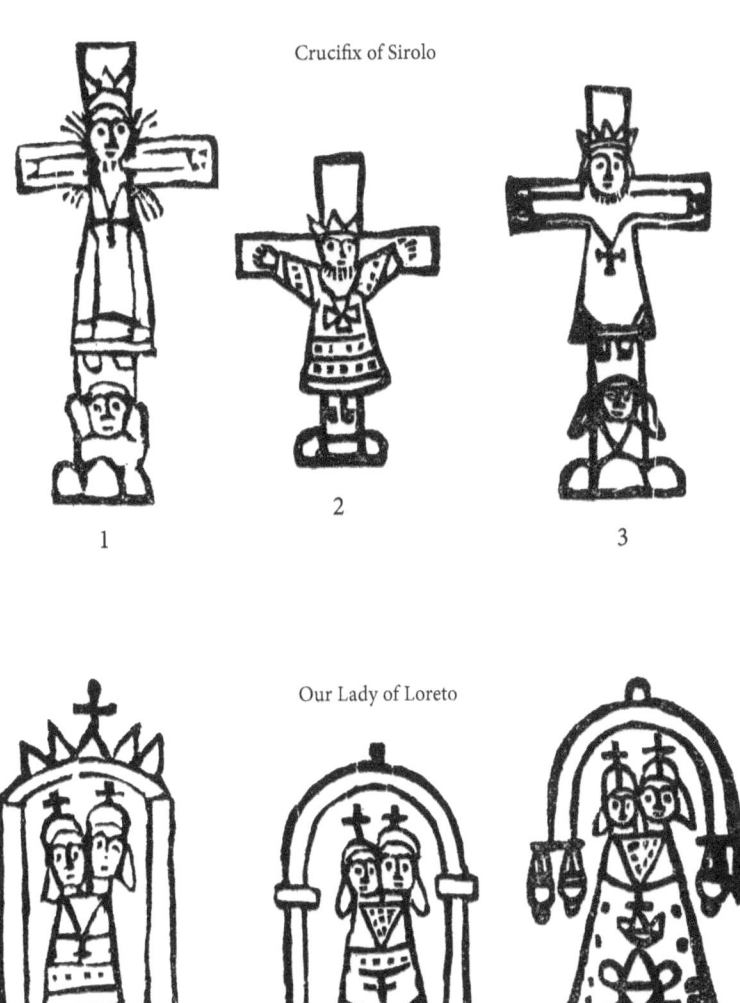

Crucifix of Sirolo

Our Lady of Loreto

VARIOUS RELIGIOUS TATTOOS

Figures IX

Madonna of good advice or of Genazzano. *

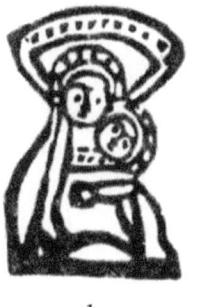

1

Queen of the sky

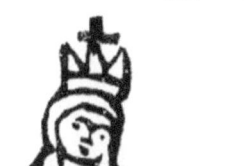

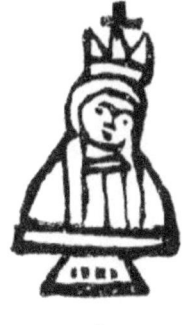

2

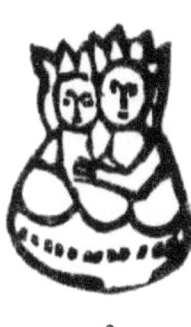

3

Madonna del Carmine

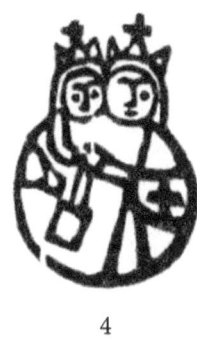

4

Emblems of the Passion

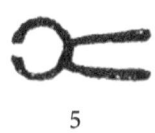

5

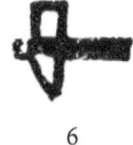

6

Globus cruciger

7

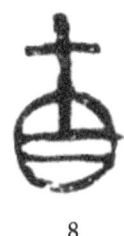

8

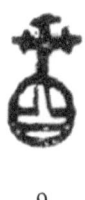

9

* The legend says that she appeared painted in Genazzano in the church of the Augustinians: the band and the stele depicting the rainbow as a sign of peace for good advice.

VARIOUS RELIGIOUS TATTOOS

Figures X

Passion of Jesus
with its symbols

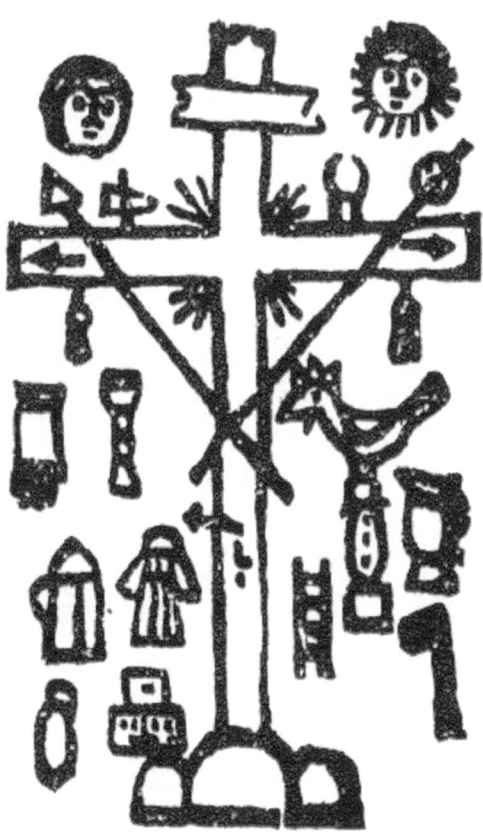

1

VARIOUS RELIGIOUS TATTOOS

Figures XI

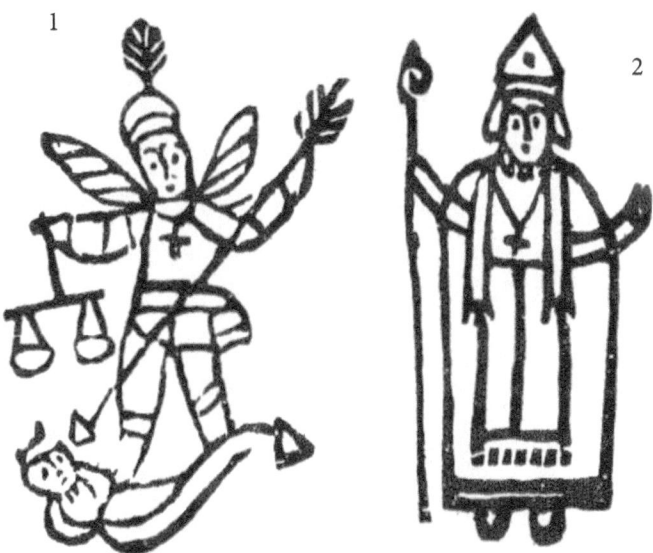

1 — Saint Michael archangel who kills the dragon

2 — Saint Emidio Bishop, protector of Ascoli Piceno against earthquakes

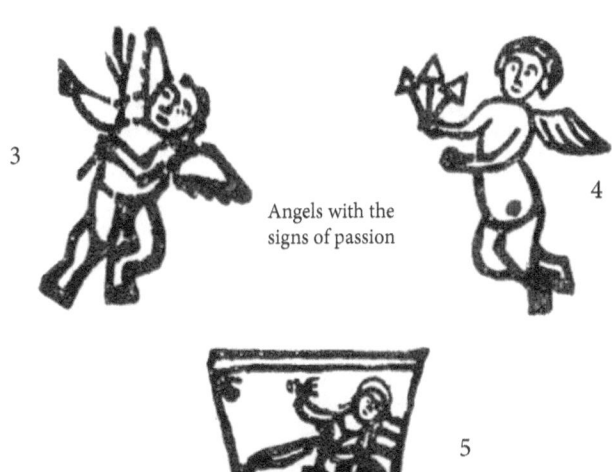

3, 4 — Angels with the signs of passion

5 — Santa Filomena discovered in the catacombs of Rome

LOVING TATTOOS

Figures XII

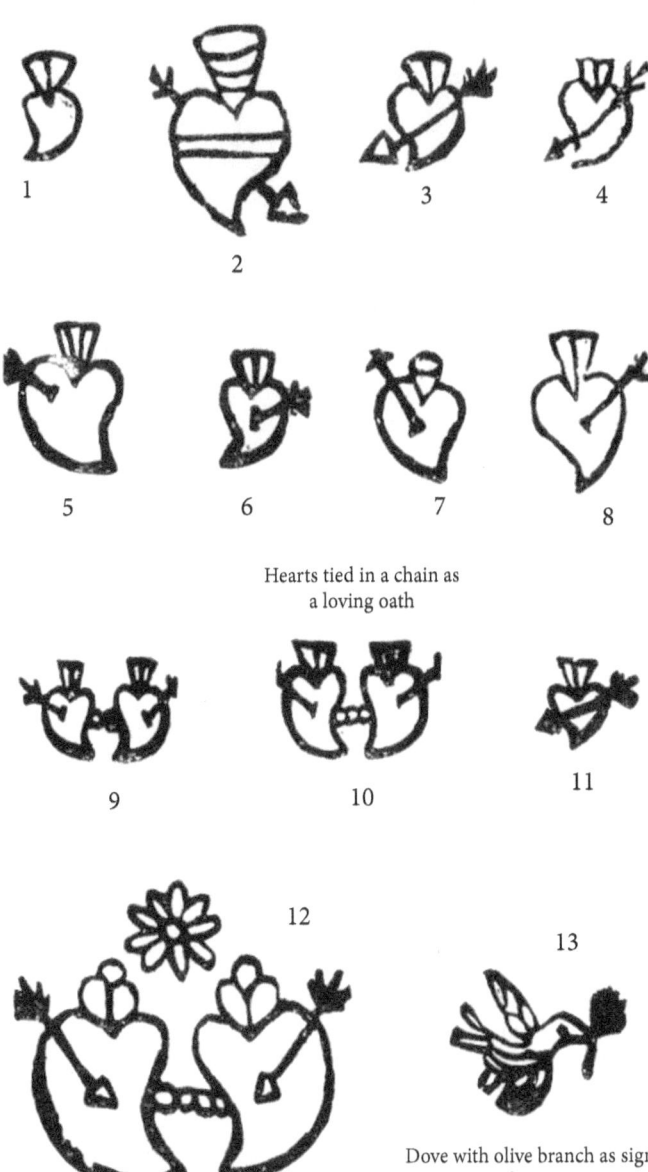

Hearts tied in a chain as a loving oath

The star (flower) could indicate the love of a sailor

Dove with olive branch as sign of peace

VARIOUS TATTOOS

Figures XIII

Tattoos of young brides, according to:
"The Word became flesh and dwelt among us"

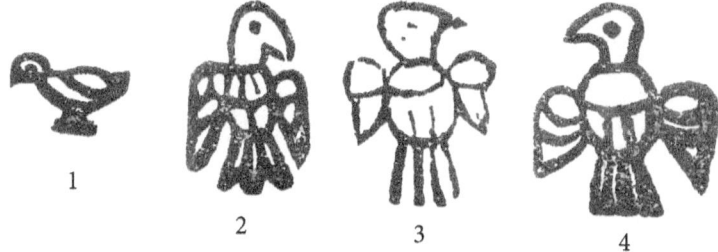

1 2 3 4

Sailors tattoos

Widow's tattoo
Memeto Mori

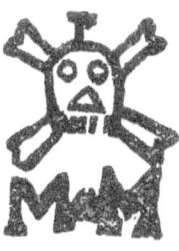

5 6 7

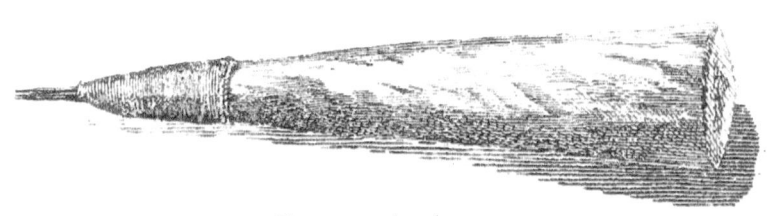

Three-pronged steel pen
with which the tattoo was practiced

BIOGRAPHY

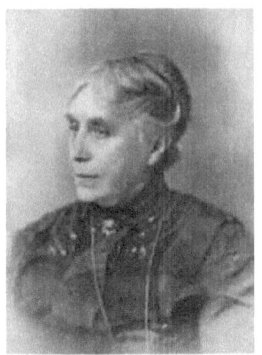

Caterina Pigorini Beri was born in 1845 in Fontanellato (PR). She was the daughter of the doctor of the her bith place and sister of the famous paletnologist Luigi Pigorini. She conducted the studies as self-taught. She became a teacher of several female schools, including those of San Paolo and Macerata, after which she was appointed director of the Royal Normal School and of the Women's College of Camerino. In this city she married the mayor and lawyer Antonio Beri.

She was the author of several writings, novels and interesting monographs on the traditions of some Italian regions, among the most important *Costumi e superstizioni dell'Appennino Marchigiano* (1889) (Costumes and superstitions of the Marchigiano Apennines) and *In Calabria* (1892). After a long illness that had struck her in 1915, she died in Rome in 1924.

www.ingramcontent.com/pod-product-compliance
Lightning Source LLC
Chambersburg PA
CBHW030506220526
45464CB00006B/2680